LOOK
AT
YOUR
EYES

LOOK LOOK LOOK
LOOK LOOK LOOK
LOOK LOOK LOOK
LOOK LOOK LOOK

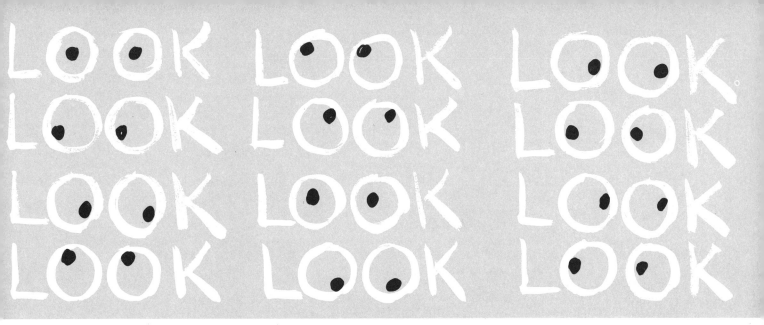

A Let's-Read-and-Find-Out Book™

LOOK AT YOUR EYES

by PAUL SHOWERS · *Illustrated by* PAUL GALDONE

A Harper Trophy Book

HARPER & ROW, PUBLISHERS

Let's Read-and-Find-Out Books™

The *Let's-Read-and-Find-Out Book*™ series was originated by Dr. Franklyn M. Branley, Astronomer Emeritus and former Chairman of the American Museum-Hayden Planetarium, and was formerly co-edited by him and Dr. Roma Gans, Professor Emeritus of Childhood Education, Teachers College, Columbia University. Text and illustrations for each of the more than 100 books in the series are checked for accuracy by an expert in the relevant field. The titles available in paperback are listed below. Look for them at your local bookstore or library.

**LOOK
AT
YOUR
EYES**

When my mother shops, I wait for her in the car.
I do not mind because I have things to do.
I watch the people go by.
I watch the cars.

1

Sometimes I look in the car mirror.

I like to make faces at myself.

Sometimes I play a game with the mirror.

I sit up straight and lean forward.

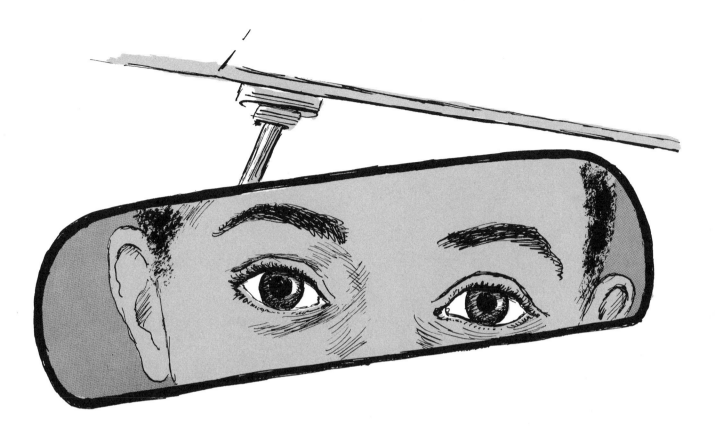

I lean close to the mirror.
I can see only my eyes.
My eyes are looking at my eyes.

I don't mind waiting when mother shops;
  I don't mind being alone.
I don't mind waiting when mother chats;
  I have a game of my own.
When mother's inside
  Buying cabbage or cake
Or trying on dresses
  Or ordering steak,
I really don't care how long it may take,
  For I have a game of my own.

It is fun to play my game with the mirror.
My friend Bill plays it, too.
He takes a mirror and looks at his eyes.

What does he see?
His eyes are blue.

My eyes are brown.

What color are yours?

Are they blue

or brown

or gray?

8

Bill looks at his eyes again.
There are eyebrows over them.

There are eyelashes around them.
The eyebrows and eyelashes are made of little hairs.
They keep dust from falling in his eyes.

Eyes have eyelids, too.
Eyelids are like window shades.
They close down over your eyes and keep out
   the light.
Then you can go to sleep.

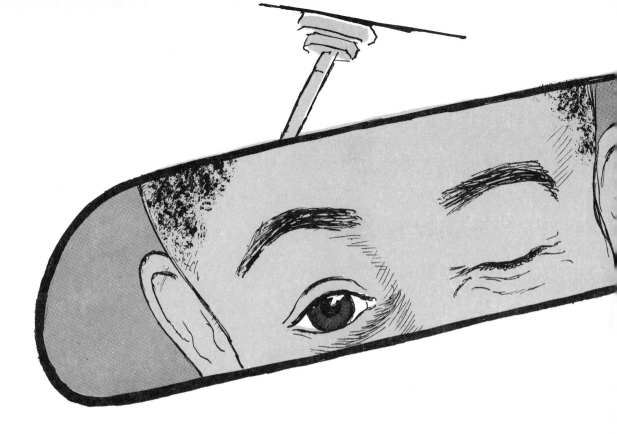

I like to look in the mirror
    And see what my eyes can see.
I like to blink and watch myself wink
    And look at my eyes look at me.

When there is a lot of water in your eyes, you have
  tears.
You do not have to cry to make tears.

Tears come when the wind blows hard.
Tears come when it is very cold.
Tears are good for your eyes.
They keep them warm. They keep them clean.

Your eyes are shiny.

That is because they are wet.

There is always a little water in your eyes.

The water keeps your eyes clean and makes them shine.

Get close to the mirror again.
Look in the middle of one
   of your eyes.
Do you see the black spot?
The black spot is called the pupil.

Sometimes it is small.

Sometimes it grows big.

Did you ever watch the pupil in your eye change
 its size?
This is how I do it.
I close my eyes almost all the way.
I keep them open so I can see just a little.
I count to ten.

One—two—three—four—
  up to ten.
Then I open my eyes wide.
I watch one pupil in the mirror.
It grows smaller as soon as I open my eyes.

Why does the pupil change its size?

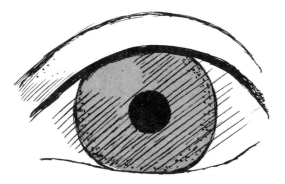

The pupil is a little round window.

It lets the light into your eye.

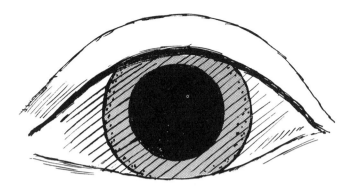

When your eye needs a lot of light,
the pupil gets big.

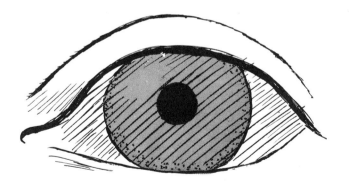

When your eye needs only a little light,
the pupil gets small.

Your pupil gets big
    when you are in a dark room,
    or when you are outdoors at night.
Then your eye needs all the light it can get.

Your pupil grows big to let in every bit of light.

Your pupil is small
    when all the lights are turned on,
    or when you are outdoors in the bright sunshine.
Then there is plenty of light to see by.
Your eye does not need so much light.
Your pupil gets small.
It keeps out the light that your eye does not need.

When I am waiting in the car, I look at other people's
   eyes, too.
Here comes Bill. He has his dog Buster with him.
Bill has big blue eyes. They look happy.
When Bill smiles, his eyes smile, too.

Buster has big brown eyes.

But Buster's eyes look sad.

Even when he is happy, Buster's eyes are sad.

Buster is a happy dog.

Buster likes to play.

But Buster doesn't know how to smile.

His face wasn't made that way.

I don't mind waiting in the car for my mother.
I play games. I watch people.
Most of all, I watch for my mother.

At last I see her in the crowd.
Her arms are full of bundles.
She sees me in the car.

She does not wave when she sees me.
She has too many bundles.
But her eyes smile at me.

That is what I like to see best.
I like to see my mother's eyes when they smile at me.

ABOUT THE AUTHOR

PAUL SHOWERS is a newspaperman and writer. He began as a copy editor on the Detroit *Free Press* and later worked on the New York *Herald Tribune.* He spent the war years in Japan, where he was a sergeant on the staff of *Yank,* the Army weekly. After a brief stint on the New York *Sunday Mirror,* he joined the staff of *The New York Times,* where he is assistant travel editor.

Mr. Showers was born in Sunnyside, Washington. He received his B.A. from the University of Michigan. He now lives in Brooklyn, New York.

ABOUT THE ILLUSTRATOR

PAUL GALDONE is considered one of the outstanding illustrators of children's books. He studied at the Art Students League in New York and with George Grosz, and he spent his spare time sketching from life in parks, zoos, subways, and streets, and doing New England summer landscapes on his vacations.

Mr. Galdone is a native of Budapest, Hungary. He now lives in Rockland County, New York, with his wife and two children.